AF244794

Incomer

Also by Bonnie Proudfoot

Household Gods (2022)
Goshen Road (2020)

POEMS

Incomer

Bonnie Proudfoot

Shadelandhouse
MODERN PRESS

LEXINGTON, KENTUCKY

A Shadelandhouse Modern Press book
Incomer
poems
Copyright © 2026 Bonnie Proudfoot
All rights reserved.

For information about permission to reproduce selections from this book,
please direct inquiries to permissions@smpbooks.com, or
Permissions
Shadelandhouse Modern Press, LLC
P. O. Box 910913
Lexington, KY 40591

Published in the United States of America by:
Shadelandhouse Modern Press, LLC
Lexington, Kentucky
smpbooks.com

Printed in the United States of America
First edition 2026
Shadelandhouse, Shadelandhouse Modern Press,
and the logo are trademarks of
Shadelandhouse Modern Press, LLC.

ISBN: 978-1-945049-65-1 (paperback)
ISBN: 978-1-945049-66-8 (epub)

Library of Congress Control Number: applied for

Cover art: Mark Hackworth
Author photo: Dan Canterbury
Cover and book design: iota books

For my mother

Contents

i

Location

He held one side of the rope, I held the other,
my legs rusting into the ground in a steel mill town,

popping tabs off cans of Stroh's. All the walls
had ticking clocks, all the bathrooms lines of coke,

and him, up to his knees in sweetgrass,
sparrows at his shoulders, hair and beard

as rosy as dawn, tin flute whistling Celtic tunes
and murder ballads. A lesson in location.

Oh, said my dad, *seen one tree, seen them all.*
Oh, said Uncle Bob, *how are things in Virginia?*

Each time I tugged back. *It's West-by-God-Virginia,*
and Uncle Bob would say in boot camp he ran across

a fellow from Richmond, pretty sure. Kind of
a yokel but give you the shirt right off his back.

Almost Heaven

When I said I was willing to throw everything into that fire,
the fire heard me and laughed. —"Willing," Alison Luterman

It could've been a movie set. Woods gave
way to a clearing, clapboard farmhouse,
porch swing, silver maple with rose-tinged
leaves. I thought that love, a garden,
a horse that pushed its pink muzzle into
my grassy palm, and the promise of land,
a backdrop he and I could paint together
would be all I'd ever need. Almost

heaven, until two of his brothers drove up,
a doe strapped to the roof of the car, her body
hollowed out, eyes holding less light than
chunks of coal, tongue lolling. They spoke
past me, *grappling hook, block and tackle,*
backstrap, passed jars of golden whiskey.
The wind flexed its muscles, the carcass
swayed from the rafters, curled into itself,

an inverted question mark. Rifles
leaned against the woodbin. Blood-stained
boots dried on the rug. Somewhere
a donkey brayed like Hank Williams
about its lonely life. Bats swept the sky
until blackness consumed it all. From
the porch swing, night folded stiff wings
over my eyes. Threshold of rough-hewn
slats. How to carry myself across.

A Brief History of Wetzel County

Here is a hill, a trail,
shale rocks crumble into earth
when I step on them,
canes of multiflora rose tug
my legs, arms, neck, face. Here
fog hugs the valleys,
autumn sun dips behind
the ridgeline before 3:00,
stumps of chestnut trees
are wider than any
living trees, squirrels
hide in oak branches.

Here Lewis Wetzel, *born
in 1764 on the South Branch
of the Potomac, resolved
to kill as many Indians
as possible.* Here I stumble
over rusted steel pipelines,
find pylons from drilling rigs
and gas wells. Skid roads
from loggers are lined
with mountain blueberries,
tiny, sweet, and tart. Thick vines
of Virginia creeper and poison ivy
dangle from the tree canopy
like broken tightropes.

Here Lewis Wetzel *was the first
to volunteer when it came*

to hunting down Indians.
Beside the trail, I bend
to scoop up a perfect
flaked slate arrowhead.
Under a blackberry bush
a copperhead watches
and never even flicks
its forked tongue.

Apology, April

I wish I could arrive on time,
but there is silver in the clouds
this morning. The earth seems
to move when the wind blows,
and the stones on the walk
somehow shine. Don't
get me wrong, I am
grateful for good company
and for good solitude. I am
grateful for the crabapple
that bloomed first in the row.
Usually, nothing comes
that easy. I am always
afraid that I will run out
of time. Clues abound,
but I still have no idea
what makes a mushroom
rise from the leaf-strewn
ground. I can't even find
that pocketknife I let slip,
now each old tool has
more weight. I am grateful for
the way deer travel the woods
across steep hillsides, firm paths,
and footholds. It's the dampness
of this valley, the warmth in sudden
pockets of air, the honeycomb
that washed up along the bank
of the creek. How it smells
like wildflowers and rain.

Pocket Fisherman

Take a kid who grew up in a city, put her
next to a pond with a pole, and soon enough,
she will catch a fish and not know what to do
with it. A Popeil Pocket Fisherman, a catfish
as long as my arm. What would my mother do,
I wondered, as a girl needs to look to
tradition, which felt right and felt wrong,
because this fish had been swimming along.
I was the one holding the red plastic reel.

The Fannie Farmer Cookbook stated,
Clean and skin: one catfish. I recalled
poached salmon, stuffed flounder,
neat filets under lights on crushed ice.
I didn't know whether to begin at the head
or the tail. I didn't know how long a catfish
could survive out of water, thick gills flapping,
eyes staring, sharp barbed whiskers, bony plate
on its neck that defied serrations of a knife.

Some things no book can teach, how
not everything that's given is free,
not a bottom-feeder from a pond gone
to cattails, not a snapped-together
plastic rod from a faraway uncle
who probably never expected it to be used.
It took about three hours to move that fish
from a living thing to a meal on a dish,
my lungs burned with every breath.
The cutting board held the reek for weeks.

"How about a little pig, sweetie?"

my father's father asked my mother's mother,
knowing, as we all did, that she kept kosher,
refused to eat pork or shrimp or drink milk with
meat, still, after marrying, my mother allowed
a few modern ways in the door, though some
things she and her mom agreed upon,
everything scratch-made, avoiding pork. Both
mistrusted commercial mixes, no precooked
or store-made, that wasn't food, ever, and it
wouldn't be fit for serving, ever. Sugar and butter
creamed, yolks beaten, whites whipped, the
Hamilton Beach mixer the only concession.

And no concessions for me or my brother
in the big unkosher city, no steaming pushcarts
hawking hotdogs. Anything could potentially crack
the thin shell. We were scratch made, so we hid
every cheat, tried to keep it all neat, and when
Mother's fingers shriveled, her body stiffened,
no one could see it, everything still shining,
and here came Grandma from across the street
down on all fours, scrubbing and waxing our floors.
Because what else have you got to show the world
who you are? Keeping kosher, but more ferocious.

Stripping Berries

Saying blackberry, blackberry, blackberry.
                    —"Meditation at Lagunitas," Robert Hass

Anyone who lives near the woods
knows how still the air feels against
skin in August, how warm, dry earth
seeps into pores, how a storm
brings the first leaves off the locusts,
how poison ivy reddens along
the path and trails narrow. It is
not a metaphor, a worn path is still
the best way to traverse the hillside,
a break in the trees will offer a clear
view, and it is one thing to be in a
figurative thicket and another to be in
an actual one, and now, suddenly
you are caught there, in brambles, as you
come upon the last of the large, seedy
blackberries, and whose berries are these,
the ones flush against the right-of-way,
whose clearing is this, where sun
reddens the back of your neck, your
fingernails turn inky from reaching
for the farthest, blackest berries,
the briars tug at your cap, at skin
on your shoulders, jab through jeans.
It's not a metaphor to say this place
has caught you, much as you've caught it,
the last tang of something you know
will be gone before you get back here,

and you think of all the times you almost
begin to forget that you have a body until
you are pierced, stitched to canes, stained
by the tug of it, until you yank your hands back
and eat as if you are just another animal
stripping berries and you got here just in time.

Tonight, Coyotes

Tonight, we're making love,
windows open to the woods,
then, a *yip-yip*,
a pause of a second or two,
and different tones,
solemn and searching
fill the room with howl.

Tonight, your hands
move my legs apart, you
find a way into me,
and it's impossible
to fathom each shifting
breath, these wails,
walls dissolve,
sound blends,
untraceable, disembodied
emerging and disappearing.

It could be hunger,
it could be joy,
not one cry,
but the whole
chorus, it moves us,
we move together,
a shaking that spirals
into the sky.

Tonight, coyotes,
then gone.
No rustle, no yip,
Everything wild
holds still.

I used to
have a body.
I used to be
so sure.

Trespasses

October, cloudless blue sky. I head to the reservoir
because it calls me. *No Swimming* is posted, but
I know a small cove, a spit of sand. Pine-scented air,
clear water, shallow at first, then a drop-off and deep.
Who I want to be feels closer with every stroke,
who I used to be peels off like clothes on the shore.

In the distance, hounds bay, maybe set loose
to hunt game, a pack on the move, off leash,
keeping tabs on each other, approaching. It hits me.
No one knows where I am. Dogs could surge
through trees. Hunters, too. I'm too far offshore
to swim back. I duck under, resurface, breathe.

In middle school assembly everyone said the
Lord's Prayer, but I never knew what words
to say, wasn't sure what it meant to pray
that way. I hoped no one saw me not speaking,
hoped my family or rabbi wouldn't find out
whose God I was supposed to be beseeching.
Oh please forgive these sins and trespasses.

Out across the open sky, hundreds of geese,
a gigantic vee, white bodies, black wings,
flapping, jockeying for position. A grand
procession, a clattering, honking racket,
headed southward toward the far shore,
noise slowly fading. No dogs. No hunters.
Something almost holy, almost within reach.

In the novel, the girl discovers a new passion,
heads back to college, becomes an ornithologist.
Or she keeps her bargain with God, goes to temple,
observes the Sabbath. In life, I swim back
to the safe and murky shore, dress, find
my pickup truck where I left it. Paradise lost,
and me, unable to grasp it when I had a chance.

Manifest Destiny

First, you hear chainsaws. Right off, you know
there's more than usual, not just homeowners
or a small crew cutting firewood. This begins

to sound like a logging operation, and it is.
It's close, too, just down the road. An echo
of bulldozer blades slamming into rock,

soil piled and sandstone crushed, bit by bit
the forest scraped for access roads, shoved away.
You never knew a machine could spin a whole tree

while it grinds off bark and branches, or that
a person could walk a mile in any direction
and still the shrill whine shatters the air.

Two months, three months, freezing rain,
snow flying, then one day the stake trucks,
flatbeds, dozers and skidders, blue porta-potty,

poplars, hickories, oaks, and maples
and acres of white pine are gone. Muddy
tracks, stacked scrap, the creek trying to find

a way through thick silt in the gully. Logs
are sold, someone's profit is tallied, but for you,
it's a ledger of loss, how red the cardinals once

seemed as they preened on green boughs, how
the sounds of the world once hushed, how rows
of jonquil and paperwhite bloomed on the berm.

Across the valley on the far hillside, your eyes find
one slender pine that missed the cull, still green.
You seek it out against the snow. You're not sure

if it will survive. More than anything you want
the world to leave it alone, so it can get on with
the business of living. Only wind can touch it now.

Rust

Now that I've come face to face with it, it's true
with the approach of winter, illusions go,

less can glow when light hangs sparse and low.
Maybe it's that ice-spot sun, sifting through

scrawny maples on the hill, guiding the eyes
down shadowed cliffs to shale slabs to bare

silver trunks of saplings, to withered, spare
ferns with crumbled leaves, nothing can rise.

Along the creek, broken limbs dangle from vines,
cast aside jars glint in the waning light, tangles

of rusting tailpipes, old mufflers, even rake tines
drawn by floods into clefts of rock at this angle.

Not hidden, not subtle. Once they're out of sight,
pastoral dreams dissolve in scant winter light.

Fubar

I knew a guy who made a living fixing cars
out of his garage, every time a caliper stuck
or a bolt seized, or he couldn't get an old muffler
loose, folks said he winged a tool through a window
in his shop and watched it shatter. I saw it for myself
one day when I walked around back to pee, sharp
slabs of glass, crowbars jutting through crabgrass,
like a flashing neon sign saying *Stay the hell away.*

Fubar, my army uncle growled when something was
fucked up beyond all repair, *far-kak-teh* my dad
said, but since he wasn't very handy, didn't try
to fix anything, it was mostly about the government.
Far-blund-jet is what I thought when something was
so broken it couldn't be fixed, say dry-rotted traces
that snapped when we hitched the horse to pull logs,
or second gear jamming on the Jeep, stalling, halfway
up the hill in thick mud, frozen groceries melting,
kids hungry, winding out first until it screamed.

In Yiddish, we whined to God. *Oy vey iz mir* went
only so far, *oy gevalt,* a little further. When snow piled
over our fence and goats trotted free, or water froze
in the gas line, the heat quit, you said *cunt, bitch, whore,*
like you needed to lash out at the women in the world.
And I backed off with each word you hurled, more proof
of female betrayal. We were two trees, rooted
in different soil, shoving each other out of the way
for the warmth of the sun, but it always got colder,
all our stuff broke at least once. But like that mechanic,

who poured a shot of Jack, cut new panes of glass
then got back to it, even if it took all day, you found
a way to fix each *far-kak-teh* thing, keep it all
going, back turned to the shatter and clash,
middle finger raised to all the powers that be.

Lesson

My mother placed the boneless breast
between two pieces
of wax paper, pounded it with the points

of a meat mallet, squat flesh resisting
as if alive,
then meat beginning to spread

wider, longer, shape breaking down.
*This is how
you soften it*, she said. She wasn't afraid

to use force. When her fingers curled
and calcified,
and she could no longer slap my cheek

with a swift hand, she took a hairbrush
to me for backtalk,
but I did not get softer. I got tough.

And when a wildness came over my son,
I remember
pulling back my arm, then stopping.

The world is already too tough.
He needed to be
tender to learn this for himself.

White Pony

From the barn I saw him, as if asleep,
but frozen already, legs splayed,
no cloud of breath, no warmth left.
He was old when we got him, nearly thirty
judging by wear on his teeth, a lifetime
of grinding. He'd been a coal mine pony
and lost his right eye, the socket healed
into a pink fist of scar tissue, the other eye
pale blue with a dark gray center, bloodshot,
pink lashes, a short white mane, a small
round white belly that sagged like an
unmade daybed without springs, his spine
a line of rocks in a shallow stream, his withers
a shaggy snowy hillock. We called him Cyclops,
why not? Saddled him up at birthday parties
and sleepovers. Unlike our other pony,
he never tried to buck or shy. We led him
around the paddock or set him out to
graze, watched him outside in the rain,
the snow, pink lashes barely blinking, tail
flicking flies, pink hooves smaller than my palm.
I used to picture him hunched in some tunnel,
carting wagons of black sooty rock, keeping
his head down. A small thing, glowing. He
made it out. We waited until the ground
thawed, started digging not far from the barn
where the hillside sloped away. It could've
been half a day, piling stones and clay, then
we hitched up the other pony, and guided
the traces as he dragged the small white stiff

shell of his only friend. One gold pony, sides
heaving with a weight barely possible to know,
one white one, shut eye toward the ground,
open eye staring empty at the sky.

Doorway to Nowhere

Because they were perfect in their own way,
      these mutts we found or maybe they found us
because they had eyes of clarified butter
because their noses were called to dirt
because of their fur, coats whose motes
      we inhaled, swapped essences with,
because they found each other in life
      like sisters of soul
because each time the clay was so dense
      and the days were so hot and the only sound
      was the mattock as it chopped through roots of hemlock
because it felt like duty
      to descend downhill through the woods to the creek
      and heft slate stones
because daffodils will grow
because daffodils are blooming now
because a grave is a doorway that opens to nowhere
      or to a place of myth and dream
because there is no school for letting go.

Occupied

You couldn't call it earthshaking, exactly,
what happened when the child was eight,

no quake, not even a tremor, no, it's when
a mother has been nothing but

a tap brimming water, and then she
no longer needs the child to drink.

Instead, she wakes up one morning
unfurnished, as empty as bare walls,

as solitary as dark polished floors. Maybe
there's a ceiling fan spinning, spinning,

maybe there's a child outside, playing,
occupied; or maybe the fresh-cut grass

smells sweet and green when the wind pushes in,
maybe she says, *I can live with this*

emptiness. Maybe we can all begin to live.

Perseids

Because the night is alive with lamps!
　　　　—"In Spite of Everything, the Stars," Edward Hirsch

Tonight the stars keep their distance.
We stretch our necks, on our backs
in the bed of the pickup.

We curse the haze, the clouds, the moon
spotlighting the night sky too bright. Out
in the field, horses snort, crickets grind

the minutes away, my son's breath slows
down, he is warm in my arms. At the creek,
a bullfrog twangs like a banjo. It starts.

David says *whoa,* he sees one flash past.
But I was watching a bat shoot out
toward the moon, circle back.

We are surrounded by everything
night, everything softly glowing. A cloud
stipples the moon, dapples into patches.

David sees the next one, too. I see
the top of the ridge, medium gray,
the black cutout shapes of trees,

silver mist on the hilltop soft
as smoke. We are low in the bowl
of the sky, slow clouds flow. David sees

the third meteor streaking earthward,
but a whip-poor-will calls and calls.
I have been waiting all my life to rise.

Lake or River

We shoveled coal
off the side of the road,
watched smoke rise
off the register,
staining walls, arms,
sleeves of shirts,
never washing clean.

I never realized there were
so many rules.
It broke me to break them.

The way a garden, so soon,
turns to grass and weeds.
When is the last chance?
Is there a sign that flashes?

Once we had four Muscovy ducks.
He butchered three.
The fourth was gone the next morning.

I liked to picture it, waddling
from small creek to bigger creek,
to a lake or a river.

You never know.

Deer

Deer, I write this because it's hunting season, and parked along shoulders
of gravel lanes are pickup trucks with empty gun racks. Men in blaze-orange
vests, rifles, shell boxes, and lunch pails lean against camper tops or tailgates,
stare when I run by. I keep my pace, past a shotgun house sagging from
subsidence and sunk into the hill, where a gaunt pit bull, incapable of
holding more than one thought, lunges against his thick chain each time
he sees me. I skirt a wide puddle where the creek spills over its banks,
a cat carcass against the berm, once recognizable by its white paws, now
just a tawny shape, disarranged. The road narrows, and I come upon you.

Deer, last week as I ran a paved road behind the high school, I heard a burst,
a crack, an echo, a whistle beyond my ears. It stopped me mid-stride. My heart
pummeled my rib cage. I turned, saw movement in drawn blinds on the porch
of a house. I took the stairs two at a time. I didn't have a chance to knock. Two
shirtless teenage boys, soft white chests, gray sweats, stood in a doorway framed
by dim fluorescent kitchen light. Before I could speak, the taller one began to
apologize, said he didn't know it was loaded, behind him, the shorter one nodded, his
eyes pale blue ping-pong balls, bobbing between his brother and me, as if I was the
one who had a rifle, as if I'd pointed it at him. They begged me not to tell their father,
an art teacher at the high school. I didn't. But I tell you, Deer, browsing in tall purple
raspberry canes beyond the creek, that they drew a bead on me, they tracked me
through sights on the barrel as I ran, one of them pulled the trigger.

Deer, I'm not sure if you're a doe or a buck. I see a shaggy white tail, a tawny rump
as you bound into a thicket at the brink of the woods. Deer, death comes
at us. You might sense this more than I do, how you know you must eat more
because days are cold, or how you hear feet strike the road, my panting breath,
way before I see you. I don't have to say anything, but I think, *Run*, Deer, before
hunters in the woods head down to the road, or hunters on the road head up to
the woods. *Run now*, while you're still strong, and I've given you a fair start.

Elegy for Fannie Farmer

In the yard, peach trees line the field,
the road snakes downhill, then drops
out of sight beyond the ridgeline, west,
toward the setting sun. Chickens roost

for the night, a few yards into the woods
a sow and piglets root and grunt. Light
stripes the lawn in long diagonals, seeps
across the windowsill. Watch her

in the kitchen, she raises children,
keeps them safe, plants a garden,
yanks out weeds, wills it to grow. Watch
her study *The Fannie Farmer Cookbook*,

check how to sterilize jars for canning,
memorize diagrams of cuts of meat,
note the correct serving temperature.
The yearling pig stares into her eyes,

then the man shoots it. Is that how
it is supposed to work? Yes,
others have been here, too, they
knew what to do. Chickens race over,

follow to the slaughter. Each time,
eyes dull, the distance less
than a weightless breath. Heat stays
in flesh. Blood stains dark brown.

Here's a chopping block, a meat saw.
She used to think that she could do
anything, be anyone she willed herself
to be. Look, here's photos,

peach trees in bloom, sun that streams
across the yard. She's at the window,
holding on for dear life, light
so bright, kitchen so clean.

Hit or Miss

Maybe it's the accidental, the way
we can't see the future, even if we play

by the rules. Maybe we quit needing illusions
or set aside ever-after conclusions.

So I might have guessed after he left
I wouldn't find any measuring spoons, but I set

about making coffee, estimating beans by eye,
spying a filter under last Sunday's *Times*.

Beside the pond, a pair of mourning doves
scratched up dust, bees forayed into foxgloves.

The coffee was feeble but fine. And there wasn't
a bit of use in reading old news, the present

undid the pundits, predictions once provident
and smart, but from where I sat, way off the mark.

Thanksgiving at the Soup Opera

I can't remember when I first learned to eat,
but I remember taking my babies off the breast
and hoping they got enough nourishment
from the scraps of peas and pulverized sweet potatoes
that they crammed between their smacking lips.
Say aaah, I'd say, opening my mouth, too;
I had to open wide and chew each time I put
a spoon to their lips. I wanted them to trust,
to know that someone would provide. *More*,
they'd say when they were old enough to talk,
and *mine* when they didn't want to share,
licking their lips, grinding food between gums.

I am reminded of this at the Soup Opera,
when I see folks who choose soup
and dip day-old bread to soften crusts.
Where else can they go but here? Outside
an ambulance screams, waiting for drivers
to clear the road. This is Fairmont Avenue,
downtown Fairmont, West Virginia. No one lives
in the mansion on the hill. We all wake to the
*Six O'Clock Mine Report. Farmington won't work,
Martinka won't work.* We all watch the sun sink
earlier each day. Icicles hang like spikes from
gables between buildings, doorways are nailed
in plywood, windows are blank with brick.

Today, like yesterday, I talk to Sue about
how our boys are grown and gone,
how the town's spirit seems to have slipped

through the shaky hands that line up here. Her
family's farmhouse caved in from mine subsidence,
she can't stand the air in the new trailer,
the bottled water they dole out. *It don't seem right.*
We keep an eye out for Betty, her shock
of white hair and thick hands. There was the
vague way the newspaper announced her son's death.
We're almost glad her husband went first. Jim
used to roll his oxygen tank through the door, hold her
coat and purse, pull out a chair for her to settle into.

Church bells strike noon, folks stop in, fill long tables
to eat donated food, some murmur, some sigh, some
hold babies or small children, while I cut onions,
potatoes, open cans of stock, give thanks for the smells
and noises of the kitchen. We don't ask questions,
we watch the sudden shimmer of sun on broken
glass on the curb, fake candles flicker on tables.
We wonder if things can get better, one onion
at a time. We hold on hard to memories, see
faces in the rearview mirror, like my boys in
the back seat, sweet and shining, always.

High Water

*

There has been a town
surged under,
on this road
beside the wide river,
this river that wouldn't stop
widening, rising,
houses stand
gaping, giving over,
front doors and clapboard siding
gone, wide porches gone,
couch cushions dangle
from branches of trees.

*

In this town it's all
headed west, like something
you can't catch,
like the already gone train,
silver clouds brighter
than the flat black cutouts
of house or hill.

*

How gray this brightness
we call sky, how black
this blackness
we call water.

*

Under a streetlight
splinters of rain.
Beside the tracks
a small boy
in black rubber boots
in a shallow puddle
stomping.

La Brea

In a Los Angeles park, dark bones of animals surface,
preserved in tar for 38,000 years. In Perry County, Ohio,
coal mine fires were intentionally set and have burned
beneath the earth for 130 years. Nearby, well water
is warm enough to brew tea, but who would drink it?

In the smoldering blackness, 82 miners buried
in the Millfield cave-in share stories of methane leaks
with men underneath the Upper Big Branch slag pile.
You can walk the woods and see dusty smoke
drift out from the damp hillside. Do timber-
rattlers nest in the warmed mineshafts?

Now injection wells and evaporation stations
line the roads like altars to extinction, gas flares
of gold shimmer in the dusk. Layers of clouds stand
apart from the sky but are still sky. We've heard that
oil and water do not mix, yet here they might do that.
This dark heat, like blood behind our breath,
it seeps into us, like how we hug our pets closer
while coyotes wail but still keen to that shrill sound.

Will anyone love this place when there is
no longer anything to extract? Never mind how
wind slams sheet metal, a rush of gas ticks
against the pipeline. This fractured stone, those
uneasy bones stained with age, they may still break
this twice-wounded clay, may yet defy the grave.

Out-of-State Plates
  (for Mary)

Weeks after the surgery, after the sling
came off and after the stitches started
to dissolve in layers of epidermis
under her breast, the radiation began.

After that, chemo for a year,
as soon as she can take it. *What
doesn't kill you makes you stronger*
say some, folks who never watched

this kind of cure. Teflon in the water,
cattle belly up, no one wants to admit
exactly how all this shit got into
everything, but now it is seeping,

and hurt expands from the streams
to bare mountaintops where we really see
the scene of the crime. Giant drills buzz
in the night and someone's tap drips poison.

It is a growing game of chance, but we
are playing with a rigged deck,
the dealer holds all the cards.
On the way to Fairmont, leaves fall

and Route 50 burns, license plates
from Texas and Oklahoma blast past.
Under the earth, the ground shakes,
just out of sight, the land is pocked and cracked

like a scar. What doesn't make you stronger
can also kill you. It will not be pretty.
At the gas station, everyone talks about
the pipeline as if it is the Yellow Brick Road.

Road Map

It's not the denial of pretending
you're not listening for the phone
to ring, a text to bing, of trying not
to wait for a late-again lover
to arrive. Don't go there. It's not
like there's anything to do
or not do. Or like the universe
has picked anything out for you.
It's what you might feel when driving
back, say, from Charleston, WV,
on a strange road at night, and
you haven't passed any towns
or house lights for miles. Here
there's no signal, maybe you missed
a sign. Maybe you pass a roadside diner,
a neon flash, lanky shadows of men
in the gravel lot stand beside
large trucks, smoking, almost frozen.
It's drizzling, foggy, the road follows
a river, glints of water flow onto
the lanes. You wonder if your car sounds
strange, you wonder whether to pull over,
but don't trust the motor not to stall,
can't decide to slow down or speed up.
Then, an animal races across the road,
a mink? a cat? toward an oncoming car,
and you do slow down. The car's taillights
vanish, the animal struggles to its feet,
its back is certainly broken, but it tries
to return to your side of the road,

small legs scuttering, each pulling

in a separate direction. You see it gain

the median, sink into grass. It's not like

you're having a conversation

with the universe, or like this

is a road map to oblivion.

You know where you are.

You are here.

New 2 You

I'm in the shoe section of New 2 You,
and it's a real Cinderella story. Everyone
wants shoes that are too narrow or too
small, knockoffs of designer sandals

next to well-worn clogs, sneakers shaped
like other people's feet. Next aisle, a mother
fills a bag with children's toys, glossy or scuffed,
a horse-drawn coach missing only one wheel,

a sippy cup with a pink fairy, her wand
an explosion of stars. Anyone can buy
a sepia-toned wedding photo, framed
in silver with a sliver of a chip in the glass.

Clerks shuffle through aisles, arrange
used prom dresses by color instead of size,
while I look for the blue tags, 50% off, but
only regulars know how to find those deals.

Once upon a time we believed in dazzling
threads of dreams, but in this place, it feels
a little like half-past midnight. You can't
expect too much, but sometimes you do

get lucky. Tonight, my dancing boots will
be shining, a little tight, but that's all right.

Swagger

When he showed up in running shorts and flip-flops,
a beat-up twenty-inch Stihl Farm Boss saw to cut down
my dead maple, eighty feet tall, three feet wide at the cut line,
twenty feet from my back porch, I should've sent him
back to Wood County. Bare-chested, no hard hat,
not a ball cap or goggles, unless aviator sunglasses
count, dressed to crack a cold one, catch the Pirates
from a chaise. Before he yanked the pull cord, he lit up
a spliff. Then I really wanted to double down, get him
out of my yard before someone got hurt. But I didn't,
because you, my friend, were head over heels, dazzled
by his slice of paradise on a mountaintop, four wolf dogs,
a drop-anything travel trailer and jones for adventure.
He could pedal his Specialized bike straight up
a logging trail or shove a tree trunk over with
bare hands, which he basically did, after the Stihl
got stuck, the bar jammed in the cut. The tree didn't
budge, didn't even tip or lean. You and I watched from
the relative safety of the porch while he set wedges
and spent all afternoon pounding them with a maul,
trunk swaying like it could topple in any direction.
By then, it was too late to throw him the hell out.
Isn't that how love works? When the tree pitched over
as if he'd planned it, I paid him and he took you home,
just you, him, and the wolf dogs, where I'm sure he
hefted you over a brawny shoulder and swaggered
you into his trailer. You fell hard. When you
called last month to say he had cancer, I wasn't
surprised he refused chemo, then solid food.
Just sips of water, hits of dope, fresh air. He

gave away the bike and dogs. Then he died
on that hilltop looking out at the woods. You
called him the kindest man you'd ever known.
Maybe he thought he could beat cancer. Maybe
he did. I bet he wouldn't have ended it any other way.

Run

Once I wanted to run so far away from her,
to leave her to it, the cuts of meat special
ordered at the butcher, the keeping up
of appearances despite it all, the all-

day and all-night sickbed sight of her,
the come-here-and-bring-me-something
need of her, the sick breath of her, nights
of coughing up blood, days of specialists,

the all-day and all-night rage at my father,
whose clumsy errors caused her more pain,
the nerve of him to drink too much wine
and burn the burgers when she couldn't drink

and she needed to eat the rare, the tender.
The nerve of him to leave her for that
younger woman, someone healthy with a son
who looked up to him. She used to try to

slap my cheek, couldn't even straighten out
her fingers. And now, three decades
later, let me sing the strength of hands
that could barely grip a steering

wheel, the grit and gumption to finish college,
get a job, a calling to help others. No
shortcuts to make her life easier, no
spouse to share the load, just a pacemaker,

and a few lousy nights when her gut did not
feel like it would explode, until it did.

First Day of Fall and I'm Flying

She is resting. I am leaving again.
It is not like I haven't left so many times.

This time, she has a morphine drip,
she can push a button when the pain hits.
Her hand so cold, fingers whitish blue.

At the airport, I feel like a non-native speaker,
I ache for someone to recognize. Every sign
and shop in my village is a reminder that I
still don't know how to belong.

She fit in so well, summer in the Hamptons,
the other seasons in town, in love
with every movie house and museum,
the whole city like a perfect layer cake
waiting for her at the perfect bakery.

Home, I walk this country lane, see leaves
rattle from the trees. The afternoon light
is blinding.

One child never strayed, he is near
when her chest heaves for the last time.

I'm the leaf that swirls far
from the tree. How much of a tree's pain
does a leaf hold? Oh world, made over from
the dust of the world that came before.

Suddenly a phone call, and I am back on a plane
among strangers. My eyes are closed.
I am watching her swim, it is early in the morning,
the water as light as the sky, one perfect stroke
after another, a little white swimming cap,
a small white curl of a wave.

Because it is beautiful. Because she loves it.
Because I can see myself on the shoreline.
Because I can keep my eyes closed
and hold it close.

Mockingbird

Her body tried to die
at least a dozen times
then she shot out
of the world when
no one was watching. Thief
who stole her must've got
a handful of fury, that's how
hard she hung on. She kept
that pacemaker ticking
under her skin long after
the warranty expired, wanting
more, next meal, next movie.
In Pittsburgh, while we waited
to see a heart specialist,
I pushed her wheelchair
through the Carnegie, past
Segal's mummified tightrope-walker,
skeletal Giacometti figures,
gaunt, grief-bound,
their downcast eyes. Not her.
Every gorgeous day was
a gorgeous day, she had to
repeat it, like something
in her took flight, like it was
something worth fighting for.
A gorgeous day.
Her mockingbird soul now gone,
but it won't stop calling out
in the dazzling sun. It's on
the tallest branch

of the tallest pine.
I can't see it,
but it's there, singing.

All That Stubbornly Persist

Praise wind, praise vultures on thermals,
the doe who steps out of forest shadows.
the peach tree that shouts pink, pink.

Praise the mother whose hands curl and shrivel,
who rages against the blade of time.
Praise the brave child who sits beside her,
massages her feet on the sofa at night.

Praise the clear-cut lot next door,
the scars and scabs of scraped earth,
chunks of trees, a few small shrubs, greening.
Praise the barn with its swinging door that seems
to cant into the hill, these tractors, steel wheels
rusting into the dirt.

Praise the mother who lets
her children go, trusting that they will return
in their own time. No one thought the fox
would come back given all this loss,
but guess what I saw trotting along the road
by the light of the moon?

And did I forget to look for joy?

Since She's Been Gone

I make lists, feed the dog whose toffee eyes
are question marks, feed the cat
whose smoky coat silks my throat,
feed birds who dart and scatter and
perch in bare branches that divide
an empty sky. The sun thins flimsy clouds
while the day holds its breath, icicles
melting, or are they getting longer?

For every present thing, also absence.

Regret is the catbird who crashes into
the porch window, stunned body coaxing
itself back to life, two soft gray pinfeathers
sticking to the plate glass, fluttering.

Paper Dolls

I used to sit on the floor of the screened-in porch
with my favorite cousin, Fyllis, ten years older,

watch her cut paper dolls, bodies forming
out of paper folds. As soon as I was old enough,

I wanted scissors in my hand. The best ones
were my grandmother's sewing scissors, so sharp,

I could crease paper, cut side to side to make a family
all holding hands, as I got older, cut head to head,

figures joined at the top made a star, like when
the camera looked down on the June Taylor Dancers

on the stage of *The Jackie Gleason Show*. I watched
my cousin's hands, so careful at cutting on the line,

how she knew how to fold, where to begin and end.
I wanted to see the outline, the leftover paper,

the pattern of her skirt or grain of our kitchen table
filling gaps where the dolls used to be. I love how

scissors make a noise a little like chewing, and how
my young sons made chewing faces when they

learned how to snip. I did it, too, watching them
twitch their noses, work their jaws and teeth,

and I realize I'm also talking about how
my boys tumbled loose into their lives,

linked and cartwheeling out of my doorframe.

Outlier

Outside, the chirping of birds is erased
by sirens and the latest newsfeed delivers
the latest news, the camera goes back
to school for this one. What a bitch,
some shy fifteen-year-old, his heart tethered
to his gun, uses lead for his brand of graffiti,
he wants to be a showstopper,
a level up in the (anti-) social strata,
Columbine, Sandy Hook, Parkland,
new codes for manhood. Maybe
he was always an outlier,
maybe instead of a pet ocelot,
his dad bought him a Black Friday pistol,
he posts it on Facebook the next day,
some ephemeral way to prove that
someone loves him.

In the hallway, the slaughter.
Bullets crisscross the walls,
bodies left to bleed out on the floor,
outside a classroom door,
a voice calls, *It's ok, bro,*
it's the police, you can come out now.
But the other students
have too much skin in the game,
stagger out the back window, shake. We
see the flowers, a few more crosses
on the roadway, messages of what's
at stake. Meanwhile in America,
Kyle Rittenhouse walks free,

Parkland students protest,
but some in the US Congress deny
that shooting even happened. We
will see gun sales spike before Christmas.

It's gun season here,
shots ring out in the woods,
birds become silent. Sometimes I
can't tell where the shots are coming from,
where they are headed.

From the Edge of the World

Winter again and drops of ice
crystallize on barren branches,
no sun for days, indigo light lingers,
snow squalls swirl and settle.

Ice crystals on barren branches,
emphatic pointers to time's passage,
snow squalls that swirl and settle.
How do I know who I am?

These pointers to passing time,
life's increments and indictments.
Is this how I know who I am?
I live at the end of the road.

Increments, indictments, bones
the dog drags out of the woods.
I live at the edge of the world.
The yard is littered with shards.

Bones dragged from the woods:
thigh, shin, scapula.
A past strewn with shards.
Broken scaffolding, parts without meaning.

The thigh, the shin, the scapula,
I claim it; it is all me.
Broken scaffolding, parts seeking meaning.
What is more real, memory or invention?

I claim it; it is all me.

What's more real, memory or invention?

Winter again, no sun,

light lingers indigo.

Cats, Too

Now New Year's is over, Christmas
lights are packed, and January
shows up without a sense of humor,
sky as gray as an old sock, every
frozen thing holding still, stenciled trees
outlining the edge of field and hill,
though since I hung a bird feeder
from the eaves, feral cats have found
my porch. Some perch on the railing,
gray and white, coal black, calico,
still as statues, some yowl at the door
or spat among themselves, spiked-out fur
like neighborhood punks or bandmates
who can't get along, all retreating
in sullen silence when I head outside.
Nights, the temperature dips into the teens,
days, I raise the bird feeder higher,
hang suet in cages. Now I feed cats, too,
though there is so little I do to pull them
through. And January plays like a broken
record. Mornings, finches and chickadees
slip down from bare branches, dusk,
skinny cats slink out like shadows,
everything hungry, everything waiting,
woodsmoke curling into a woolen sky.

Rocky Soil

Out of spite, I break
morning with the sky
a canopy of icy blue.
Swords of sunlight
crackle the surface of the pond,
the eagle's huge nest stands empty
at the top of the sycamore.

There's more to finding
than what I set out to look for.
There are graves here,
beneath the cedars,
they keep me company, faithful,
like hounds when they know.
And horses, chewing,
heavy horses that always seem
to need food, and buzzards,
circling the valley in rounds of sorrows,
wing feathers divided
by ridges of high mist. This texture
of life, it does not protect me
from dreams of terror. A deer
sheds its antlers, small creatures
pick the bones bare, whatever remains
even smaller insects will scratch
from this almost frozen ground.

Things that remain unbroken
still get scars. In the sky,
the slimmest shadow of a moon,

sky, then moon, then sky again,
and though each step I take
may reveal nothing
to those who come after me,
I take this rocky soil
and try to dig.

How Many Zithers

Do you want the zither?
my brother asks, and I say yes,
because it was Mom's, it hung
on the wall in the living room in Queens,
with me for my entire childhood. I
thought I'd learn to play, but
I couldn't get past the tuning,
about forty strings, twangy to tingly,
tole-painted, gold highlights, matte black,
harp-shaped, small enough to strum
on a lap. I once asked for help at
Blue Eagle Music, but no one there
had ever played a zither. I wonder
how many zithers are in Athens County.
I can't part with it, but I've placed it
deep into the bedroom closet, behind
the oversized luggage, the clothes
that are just too city. Somehow
the word *zither* reminds me
of Yiddish, of times I've thought,
but not deployed, *klutz, shemozzle,*
bupkis. I still don't know what to
hold on to. When I jostle
through boxes, no one hears
the zither play but me.

Chair

My Manhattan cousins owned a golden chair
that looked like a huge hand, maybe the god of décor.
Its seat was a palm, fingers crooked to cup a couple
of buttocks. It seemed to have risen fully formed
from thick white shag on the floor. I didn't dare
set my puny derriere on their resplendent seat.

Not like in Queens. *Cop a squat, sit the heck down,*
take a load off, everyone said, not necessarily on
any furniture. A squat could be copped on a ledge,
a car's bumper, front stoop. A chance to get the scoop,
schmooze or talk, watch kids chalk the sidewalk.

Pull you up a chay-yer, said my WV ex-in-laws,
grab you a chay-yer, or get you a set. A fireplace,
an oval rug, and four, five chairs, caned seat or cloth,
sunken or soft, La-Z-Boy or ladder-back. I never knew
whether it was an invite or a test, what they'd think
if I set myself into one that someone else liked best.

At thrift stores here in Athens, I hunted for
an armchair that fit me, or maybe added more,
a hand-me-down history, a solid line between
hand and mind, a kind of second spine.

In Chaucer's time, it had three syllables.
Cha-y-ere says the *OED*. Maybe that's how
folks spoke when time moved more slowly,
or maybe having a chair was rare, a space apart
to take the measure of your own heart.

January 28

All morning we waited, the January air frigid and clear,
Come see, I said, pointing at the TV. Your not-quite-
three-year-old body settled beside me on the corduroy couch.
You were my playmate, usually you told me who to be,
sometimes Maid Marian when you were Robin Hood,
mostly Princess Leia and Luke, but that day I called you
the first spaceman, John Glenn, while I was the first
teacher in space, Christa McAuliffe, I pronounced,
my teacher heart swelling. Then, you led me by the hand
into the capsule, we waved to school children gathered
to see the launch. Even Tom Brokaw seemed
to have his heart on his sleeve when he introduced
mission control for the countdown, the liftoff.

On our couch from a mountaintop in West Virginia,
surrounded only by the universe, we could almost see
the *Challenger* capsule head into orbit beyond the sky;
except, a jagged fork that looked wrong, and then
the waving stopped, hands covered mouths, children stood
in silence, and you looked up at me for answers
I did not have. *I'm sorry*, I wanted to say. *I'm sorry
I called you over to watch with me, that you had
to see this.* Again and again, the TV replayed the liftoff,
as if, if they showed it once more, it would go differently.

But no, a small streak of light, a speck of fire. Sometimes
it takes so long to figure out what I want to tell you,
even longer to know which words to use, and now, thirty-five years
later, divers find sets of *Challenger* tiles on the ocean floor,
like pennies dropped into an infinite well. My boy,

now a father, sometimes what you long for will
disappoint you, and sometimes what you love will rise
because of your love, and you'll rise too. All afternoon,
on our little speck of earth, death walked beside us, his
index finger waggling, a broken branch, and we did
the only thing we could, walked down the lane, gathered
warm eggs from the hens, picked up limbs the wind
scattered onto the road, scanned the empty sky for signs.

At Your Age, I Found the Blues

Does our skin hold memory
the way we held hands, looked
both ways, then moved together into

traffic? Who taught me to stop?
I saw the light change, I willed
our four legs to step together

off the curb. *Cross at the green*
not in between. What song
do you carry now, your blond curls

turned brown, your beard streaked in gray,
father to a little girl, what do you
give that she'll carry? *Rain, rain,*

she sings, *go away.* At your age,
I found the blues, some truth
that seized my throat, hung close.

Even now, I'm holding
my own heart out to the light,
to the racing ongoing world

reckoning in 4/4 time with my own
stitched life, how to unbind grief,
how much weight to bear. When you

took those first tottering steps,
when you reached for my hand
at the curb, it was all I could do

to hold you back, off you went,
moving forward faster than ever.
Rain? Yes, there will be rain.

Shock Wave
>   *(for Dan)*

No way to know when you first touched
my hand, how deep the shock wave would reach.

Next came the checklist: favorite movie,
favorite song, political party, poets, beers,

coffeehouses and bars, haunting questions,
the snore test, making up after arguing,

all rippled into that wave, modulated through
that thing that had begun to work, to be the us

part of me, to lift me into your joy,
to hold me steady, to tug me into your pain.

Once a volcano erupted under the sea
near Tonga, its wave circled the planet

for three days, a little line tacking against
an axis changing tides and air pressure.

Just another way to say blood pulses
against skin, salt on lips. This space in me

that I worked so hard to carve out, without
knowing how you would fill it. Who I've

yet to become and who I used to be.

Hot Enough

not a spark
but a blaze,
not a welding torch
but a glass furnace
molten and glowing,
heat like an express train
across the tongue
down the throat, not
Chet Baker or Stan Getz,
but Arnett Cobb, Pharoah Sanders,
not Ringo but Gene Krupa,
Buddy Rich, a box set
of surprises,
better to surrender.
Hot enough for you?
my neighbor asks.
No, of course not.
Give me ghost peppers,
Carolina Reapers,
keep that Frank's off the table,
kiss with your teeth.

The Body Holds Its Own

> *The plan is the body.*
>
> —"The Plan is the Body," Robert Creeley

There's a way the body can't repair itself, once undone,
holding what's lost or broken, making it less than one.

It's a matter of blood or bone, the shatter of the body,
this body, this place of loss, keeping what's half-done.

Palace of peculiar balance, not insubstantial, not transmuted,
found in body, fixed in body, a broken vessel, renewal unbegun.

So, for now, as Creeley says, "The plan is the body." I'm in,
with skepticism about what might be, the lure of the long run,

or memories, if we can call them that, of what could've been.
Isn't that how it works? The might-have-been meets the short-run,

the present is gone before it couldn't have possibly become.
What to connect us, then? The kiss that was the most fun,

a song lyric recalled, how this body once moved with yours?
Though now, would any music do? What if it's not in the one

plan Bonnie's body holds? A kiss lasts a long time, but not long
enough. Leave a mark. Let our bodies hold what they have done.

Mallard

My granddaughter is learning to walk,
learning to talk, too. She trundles along
sometimes holding her dad's hand,
sometimes squatting down to pick up
twigs or pebbles. *Rock*, she says, so
proud to name this. We are at the
shoreline of Mud Lake, gazing out at
ripples on the water. We want to
hurry her along, but every few steps
she spies another pebble to examine.
A lone mallard flies in, wings wide,
quacking softly, skims across the lake,
settles somewhere just out of sight.
We make our way along the path
until we see it on a rock a few yards
offshore. My son hoists his daughter
up onto the rail of a split rail fence,
where we watch her watching the mallard
who is standing on one splayed orange
foot, the other tucked up against his
body, the sheen of his coat reflecting
the sunlight, the green of his neck
and head dazzling. *Duck*, she says
and picks up her left leg, the same
one that the mallard has raised, and
stands watching, holding on to one
rail, balanced on another, sunlight
playing in her hair. *Duck*. The mallard
was not impressed. But I was. How
else, then, do we learn what

the world can teach us, but by

living side by side with it. Give

us mallards, give us toddlers,

give us twigs and pebbles,

give us a lake, and let it

show us who we can be.

Coloring Book with Secret Superheroes

This is a coloring book without lines.
This is a coloring book where Jane
wears any clothing she feels like wearing
and so does Dick, and both of them
won't carry a gun. In this book
guns aren't invented. Still, this book
is full of action figures, girl ones and boy ones,
Wonder Woman and Captain Marvel
and Doctor Strange and Harley Quinn, ones
who move in light, and ones who delight
in mayhem. All the superheroes use their powers
to keep sharp things out of babies' reach,
even though they shine. There's a secret superhero
and it is you, you can find her if you look,
this is a book that claps for you who can
almost roll over, who has never worn
a shoe, who can eat her bare feet,
who marched at six months of age,
well, sort of marched, for women's choice.

This is a coloring book that says it's ok
use all the colors, be who you are, it hopes
you see the light that shines through your light
gray eyes, a book that looks like a mirror of love,
that smells like your breath that is a mirror
of milk, that marvels at the impressionist
masterpiece that is your diaper after eating
peas and beets, and that is only something
a nana would say, yes, yes, this book
has another secret superhero, NanaMan,

who has the power to stop a gun from firing
at a supermarket or a school or a church
or synagogue, NanaMan is the conscience
of the world, or some kind of weird spirit,
don't ask me how she/he works. The book
knows that babies are born into light, they come
here with all the colors that they need, and
when all the pages are clasped together
it prays that the world does not start
taking those colors away too soon.

Flight

It was one of those times I made
it to the bus to the airport
in plenty of time, one of those
flights that felt like it might also
be on time, my love, the gate boarding
going as well as it could, checking
boarding passes, *ping, ping*, squeezing
a suitcase into an overhead, squeezing
my butt into seat B, all this a regular weight,
but not too heavy, but then the wait
begins, rain delays on the runway,
a sudden feeling that home is further
than ever, as if the present I live through
might not lead to the future I imagine,
the mask digging into my ears,
the air darkening outside, then finally
lifting off, rising into deeper darkness,
the long droning slog through the air,
then landing, glint of rain, dim fog settling
as the highway narrows, the scratch
of windshield wipers interminable,
gauntlet of deer mostly still as statues,
then home, the house dark except
for odd little digital dials, it's way past
4 a.m. now, even the pets are groggy
and you're sleeping so soundly, but
your arms open, and for the first time
in two weeks, I release the weight
of being who I imagine that everyone
needs me to be, I lie down beside you,

the air just beginning to glow, doves
starting to call the dawn, and now,
my love, I'm so light I could fly.

Because It Is Spring in Appalachia

and rain has stopped pummeling
the solar panels on the roof,
I begin noticing things.
The rush of green outside hits me

like a fanfare, the sun
sparkles in every droplet,
but then I realize the applause
I thought I heard isn't applause at all,

it's a pair of small birds pecking away
at the inside of the walls because
they decided their new nesting place
could be a small space between

the eaves. And there it is,
the outside world come home
to roost. And me, I couldn't pull
the trigger of a .22 on a groundhog

in our blueberries, I try to save the planet,
not just for me alone, but so I
can share it, but not my house,
I think. Yet that is what's happening

and here I am, hoping to return
to Aaron Copland in my mind,
while the planet has other ideas.
Like a new station on the dial,

these little syncopated taps,

calling me to act or be acted upon,

and isn't that what I wanted

from this ragged, unfinished life?

Emerald Ash Borer

And never mind about the ash trees,
each husk of a trunk silvering
roadways and ridgetops,

bark split and shrugged off,
each day another long crack
works toward the crown,

slides down to crumble
at the root line
until the trunk is so nude

woodpeckers cease tapping.
Tunnels made by hungry larvae
beneath the bark have sapped

this tree, as if one beetle
can be blamed for bringing down
ten million so far. It can

but not all at once, it seems,
as I gather jagged broken limbs
for the fireplace, winter's dry harvest.

Blame the beetle, blame
blasts of wind. The past is
what is now passed down.

A branch dangles above
our heads, as patient as a tree,
waits its turn to fall.

The Question Is Still the Wind

> *The thesis is still the wind.*
> —"Where the Circles Overlap," Ada Limón

and will branches or limbs fall
where they will and will leaves
swirl in circles, shake like a skirt,
and how hard will each blast
race across the highest edge
of the ridgeline, twirling
treetops, and how much do those
high branches sway, whether
more or fewer leaves can buffer,
whether thin or thicker trunks can
bear the strain, and will we hear
that terrible sound, like drumming
and hoofbeats and howls of
a wounded creature, or the sharp
gunshot cracking of a thick trunk
or trunks splitting, then toppling,
crushing brush, raw wood gaping
and maybe it all depends on
whether roots have found
their way deep enough into
the earth or maybe it's a mystery
whether substrate below topsoil
is shallow or deep,
the ground clay or silt or sand
and the question is still the wind
how lately storms gather
stronger and last longer,

and should these trees that you love
really be so close to your house,
and what about the birds?

Elegy for Dewey Stone

Last May, Dewey died from diabetes after
a slide into dementia, not fully, just enough
to lose nouns, verbs, to ache with the loss.
Did I mention his name was not really Dewey?
That once, hitchhiking from Buffalo to Woodstock,
someone named Louie picked him up, and
in the car was another guy named Hughie.
I'm Dewey, he said, and then he was. We
rolled joints on album jackets, listened to Santana,
and watched cartoons. He sang, *I got a black*
Magic Marker. Did I mention that once when he
was away, while I was watching his husky, she
darted across the road into an oncoming car?
I held her broken body, watched her blue eyes
go blank. Didn't Road Runner take a Magic Marker
out of his invisible pocket and draw a tunnel
into a mountain? Is that where the dog is?
Are they together, with their shining blue eyes?
Does he still stop on the sidewalk every time
a girl says, *Beautiful dog.* Does he say, *Yes,*
I know. Her name is Yahweh. I still listen to Santana.
If I had a black Magic Marker, I could block out
a portal through time and gravity, someplace between
11:30 and midnight. He called from the hospital.
It's fucked up, Dewey said. *I cry a little every day.*
I never asked whether he forgave me for killing
his dog. I never wanted to hear him say he did.
Did I mention how much we used to laugh?

Lost, a List

Sasha, our black-and-white border collie
with a friend's Brittany spaniel. We hiked
past coyote dens, flushed grouse, met neighbors,
thought about how dogs might think,
how circles could be better than corners.
They showed back up & slept for days.

Little boy Daniel on a borrowed bike.
We crisscrossed roads where drivers took
curves too quickly, searching for a blond head
barely higher than the handlebars. A blue K-car
pulled up, a man lifted a bike from the trunk,
& Daniel opened a door, said, *I got found.*

Dain is losing his marbles, my mother-in-law
mentions one Sunday afternoon from her wing chair,
teacup on the snack table, minister on TV. From
his La-Z-Boy, Dain nods agreement & I think
of the marbles I've lost, opaque, precious,
out of reach, no chance of returning home.

Holding On

We bought a crooked house
on a rolling knob
a jagged diagonal slice
of a partly wooded hilltop
a hand-dug basement and
screened-in porch,
sloping floors, un-square
rooms, walls stuffed
with faded newspapers,
yesterday's weather,
ads, and squabbles.
Slate slabs hauled
from the creek
once formed a path,
now they sink and
crumble. Outside is
always in, pebbles stick
to boot treads, and mud
to pant knees, fingernails.
Windows and doors can't be
coaxed to close, even new
ones shift shape. Us, too,
our bodies tethered
by twisted threads, the hills
and valleys of us, all
falling out of line and
falling back into it,
holding on to
less each day.

Prayer

Today, the late September breeze turns
wicked cold, and my body wants
to curl into itself. At the doctor's
I say, *I hurt here, and here,* and he says,
I don't see anything, so I don't push it,
although I feel like that person who

brings the car to a mechanic, only to find
that the noise evaporates as soon as it's
on the lift. I believe in my arms that
used to, my legs that used to. Tonight
is the first night of Rosh Hashanah,

online, from the temple that has memorial
plaques for my mother, uncle, cousins,
I will watch a cantor singing *Kaddish,*
bow my head in silent supplication
during the *Amidah,* my brother will

message me the sound of the *shofar.*
Oh new year, oh leaf swirl,
cricket song, moonrise,
rattle-clap of change,
help me to surrender,
help me to resist.

Oh, Israel

(Next year in Jerusalem —a portion of the Passover seder)

Oh, Israel, if my love is a suitcase, when I get to your house
I won't unpack, even though my mother and her mother,
my uncles and cousins are buried in pine boxes beneath
a Star of David. The rabbi wept for victims of the Holocaust,

cried for a homeland for the children of Zion. Yes, I used to feel
my chest swell open when I heard *Hatikvah,* yes, you've suffered,
people taken in sleep, in song, as they walked out of their homes.
I know you are perched on a precipice of strife. I, too, have felt

like a stranger in a strange land, my family holding our faith close
to shield us from hate or harm. Here, in the safety of my small
life, I see signs on the highway, a deer rearing up, a warning one
may careen across the road, but that isn't how it happens, not

right beside a road sign. When terror charged, you weren't
ready. I see stolen homes, stolen land. I see that hate calls out
in darkness for more hate. Gazan families starve, pick through
ashes to find bodies to bury while you shatter hospitals, shelters.

I mean blood will stick to you, Israel. You shatter us, too, we
who were raised with a dream, who held you in light every
Friday night. Two peoples, breath of one breath, voices
raised to one God. The more faith you steal, the less you'll keep.

When Gods of Morning Wake Me

Will it be the crow
        awe, awe, awe,
        praising her own beauty

Will it be the dream
        of flying home
        to my own solid body

Will it be the flash
        of light
        on the flycatcher's wing

Will it be the eyes-closed god
        who runs
        from the world,
        seeks only herself

Or the god of compromise,
        braced against the corner
        standing on her head,
        therefore, always sinking

Or will it be the wind, whose voice
        always changes, who can't help
        but tell the truth,
        always reminding me
        of what I am a part of?

The View from Where I Am Not

It looks especially inviting today, a snow-dusted
Christmas tree in Rockefeller Center, a menorah
in Central Park, but I'm on a ridgetop researching

apple grafts, whips, and scions. Experts advise
Melrose, the Ohio state apple, for our climate zone,
which was just changed from 6a to 6b. I once was

married in Roslyn, a few towns away from Melrose.
That's my only connection. A scion is what they
call a young shoot or bud from a desired variety.

When I left for college, I botched it up so badly
I needed to land a job right away. I could wait
tables, I could dance in a neighborhood bar

that advertised *GIRLS! GIRLS! GIRLS!* where
cigarettes and drinks were cheap, but I chose
driving a cab. Buffalo had so much snow that year

that taxis could whip across the streets into
anything with no harm done to the checker cab.
And that's how I knew I was cut loose. What

this view is trying to show me is I was hungry
for something to graft onto, something that wasn't
Queens. The apple tree we planted last year,

we call her Louise, might or might not make it,
her scion is Melrose, she's grafted to something native.
It's snowing again. And this tree is so tangled up

in history. I want to ask the earth not to freeze
below the graft. I want to ask it whether I have
roots here. I want to tell it I can feel the grass grow

when my son plays the banjo. No one promised
that the wound would heal underneath the tattered
burlap. I understand this ache and it understands me.

To Vincent

Again, autumn is gone too soon. Only in October
is the sky so blue, Dutch blue, Delft China blue,
and the hayfields bronze and glowing.

Do you know that as the arc of the sun lowers,
every direction on this ridgetop could be
one of your last canvases, *Wheatfield with Crows?*

Light moves fitfully through the stubble of wheat,
crows cluster in unruly flocks along the horizon,
their raucous calls speak of endings, of want.

The world wears us down despite any struggle
to resist. What is there to look to
but the landscape? Cerulean sky, tree line,

wheatfield, night gathering, bringing crows.
Oh Vincent. Maybe you spent your whole life
trying to keep those crows out of your painting,

and then one day you finally let them in.

Acknowledgments

I am grateful to the editors of the following journals and anthologies where earlier versions of the following poems have appeared or are forthcoming:

Change Seven: "How Many Zithers"

Gyroscope Review: "Trespasses"

I Thought I Heard a Cardinal Sing: "Perseids"

New Ohio Review: "Hot Enough" (nominated for Best of the Net)

Northern Appalachia Review: "Emerald Ash Borer," "High Water," "Incomer," (now titled "Almost Heaven," with substantial changes made to the final stanza), "La Brea," "Mockingbird," "Rocky Soil"

Of Rust and Glass: "Location," "Occupied," "Tonight, Coyotes"

ONE ART: "Because It Is Spring in Appalachia," "Elegy for Dewey Stone," "Flight," "The Question Is Still the Wind"

Pine Mountain Sand and Gravel: "Chair," "Doorway to Nowhere," "First Day of Fall and I'm Flying," "From the Edge of the World"

Red Eft Review: "White Pony"

Sheila-Na-Gig: "At Your Age, I Found the Blues," "Lost, a List," "The Body Holds Its Own," "To Vincent"

SoFloPoJo: "Late August," (now titled "Stripping Berries"), "Prayer," "Since She's Been Gone"

Still: The Journal: "A Brief History of Wetzel County," "All That Stubbornly Persist"

The Lyric: "Hit or Miss"

The New Verse News: "Coloring Book with Secret Superheroes," "January 28," "Oh, Israel," "Outlier"

Twelve Mile Review: "The View from Where I Am Not"

Women of Appalachia Project, Women Speak: "Deer," "Elegy for Fannie Farmer," "Holding On," "Lesson," "Road Map," "Swagger"

Notes

"A Brief History of Wetzel County" contains quotes from the *History of Wetzel County, West Virginia,* (italicized sections of the poem are from www.wetzelwv. com/about-wetzel-county).

"Apology, April" was inspired by Alison Luterman's poem "Because These Failures Are My Job."

"At Your Age, I Found the Blues" was inspired by Maggie Smith's poem "At Your Age I Wore a Darkness."

"Coloring Book with Secret Superheroes" was written after the Uvalde school shooting at Robb Elementary School, in Uvalde, Texas, outside San Antonio, Texas, on May 24, 2022.

January 28, 1986, is the date of the Space Shuttle *Challenger* disaster, a failed NASA spacecraft that killed all seven crew members seventy-three seconds into the flight.

"La Brea" is an ekphrastic poem that was inspired by the abstract artwork of Ohio artist Michael Seiler.

"Lesson" was inspired by Ada Limón's poem "The First Lesson."

"Mockingbird" was inspired by Rose M. Smith's poem "Choice."

"Outlier" was written in response to the Oxford High School shooting, Oxford Township, Michigan, near Detroit, Michigan, on November 30, 2021. Four students were killed and seven were injured.

"The Question Is Still the Wind" was inspired by Ada Limón's poem "Where the Circles Overlap."

"To Vincent" is an ekphrastic poem that responds to Vincent van Gogh's *Wheatfield with Crows*, known to be one of his last paintings.

"When the Gods of Morning Wake Me" contains a line from the poet Michael Olson.

With Gratitude

Incomer could not have taken shape without the inspiration, encouragement, generosity, and overall midwifery of Pauletta Hansel. Many thanks as well to Dick Hague, Sherry Cook Stanforth, Ellen Austin-Li, and the community created by Writer's Table, as well as Draft-to-Craft poet friends, whose kindness and dedication to poetry continue to bring me so much joy and inspiration. Thanks to my dear former Hocking College English Department colleagues in the Every Tuesday poetry group, as well as to Andy Semons, Dan Canterbury, trusted readers. Thanks to Mark Hackworth for granting permission for me to use his photograph for the cover image. Mark's photography never ceases to move me to risk more in my own work. Thank you, Trudy Hale, the Nancy Zafris Fellowship Committee, and The Porches, for your kindness and support and for the space and time needed to complete this book. And finally, deepest gratitude and appreciation to Virginia Underwood and the team at Shadelandhouse Modern Press for their assistance and professionalism and for their faith in bringing this book into existence.

Bonnie Proudfoot moved from New York to West Virginia in 1979. She received a BA in art education and English education from Fairmont State, an MA in English from West Virginia University, and an MA in creative writing from Hollins University. She was an associate professor at Hocking College, Nelsonville, Ohio, for over twenty years. Proudfoot received a fellowship in the arts from the West Virginia Department of Arts, Culture and History. She has published fiction, poetry, reviews, and essays. Her novel, *Goshen Road*, (Ohio University Press/Swallow Press, 2020) was selected by the Women's National Book Association for Great Group Reads, long-listed for the 2021 PEN/Hemingway Award, and awarded the Writers Conference of Northern Appalachia (WCoNA) Book of the Year. Her writing has been nominated for the Best of the Net and for a Pushcart Prize. Her debut book of poems, *Household Gods*, was published by Sheila-Na-Gig Editions in 2022. She lives in Athens, Ohio, and delights in the writing communities she has found throughout the region. To find out more about Proudfoot, visit bonnieproudfootblog.wordpress.com.